The Playful

Dolphins

by Linda McCarter Bridge
Photographs by Lowell Georgia

BOOKS FOR YOUNG EXPLORERS
NATIONAL GEOGRAPHIC SOCIETY

Dolphins leap and dive together as they swim through the sea.
They like to jump up in the air and splash back into the water.

Most dolphins live in oceans, but they are not fish. Dolphins are mammals and breathe air. They must come up to the surface of the water to breathe.

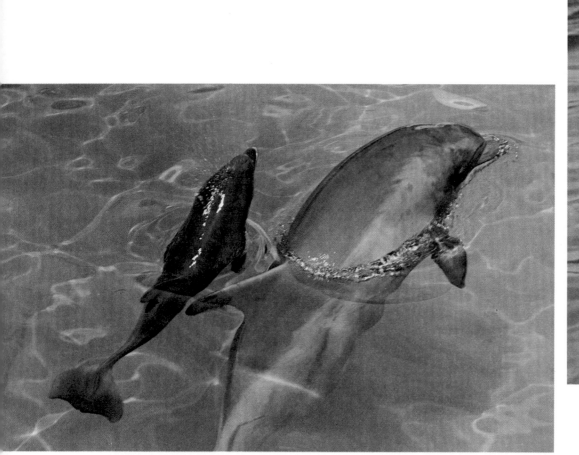

A baby dolphin bobs up next to its mother.
The baby is only three days old, but it swims
and comes up to breathe air just like its mother.
A dolphin breathes through a hole,
called a blowhole, on top of its head.

Another baby swims close to its mother underwater.
When a dolphin swims slowly, it holds its breath
just a little longer than you can.
Mother dolphins nurse their babies for more
than a year, until they learn to eat fish.

Little Mo wants to play catch with a ring.
The ring is dropped over Mo's snout. WHIZ.
Mo throws the ring up in the air with his head.

Mo likes to throw his toys to people, over and over again.
He is one year old, and he lives in an oceanarium. This is a zoo
for ocean animals where some of them perform in shows.

Whistles and fish are used
to train dolphins to do many things.
When a dolphin does something well,
the trainer quickly blows a whistle
and gives the dolphin a fish.
Dolphins like fish. They soon learn that
a whistle means they will get a tasty fish.

When a trainer points his finger, it is the signal
for the dolphin named Coral to swim away.
If she obeys, the trainer blows his whistle.
Then Coral swims back to the pole for her fish reward.
The dolphin named Flipper slides out on the deck.
He tries to get some fish while no one is looking.

This is a school where dolphins
learn to perform in shows.
A trainer is teaching
a dolphin to come to a target.
The target is a pole or his hand.
Each time the dolphin touches
the target with its snout,
the dolphin gets a prize—a fish!

Almost show time! An excited dolphin jumps in its pen.
During the day, most trained dolphins stay
in pens next to the big show pool where they perform.

Dolphins get to the show pool through a gate underwater.
When the gate is opened, the dolphins swim through it.
This is one of the hardest things to teach dolphins to do.
They do not like to swim through small, narrow places.

Two curious dolphins peek out of their pool.
It is time for fun.
Peanuts plays with water from a hose.
He catches the water in his open mouth.
Betty finds a fish in a funny place.
She quickly grabs it from her trainer's teeth.
Another dolphin uses its flipper to shake hands.
It is easy to like playful dolphins.
They seem to like people, too.

A trainer uses his hand and his foot to give signals.
When he points his finger at the dolphin, it turns around.
When the trainer sticks out his foot, the dolphin shakes its head.
Two dolphins learn to jump over a high pole at the same time.
After much practice, a strong dolphin moves its tail
back and forth in the water to tail-walk across the pool.

Up and over! Alvin, Chubby, and Flippy fly up out of the water and

over a high rope. It takes lots of practice for dolphins to jump as a team.

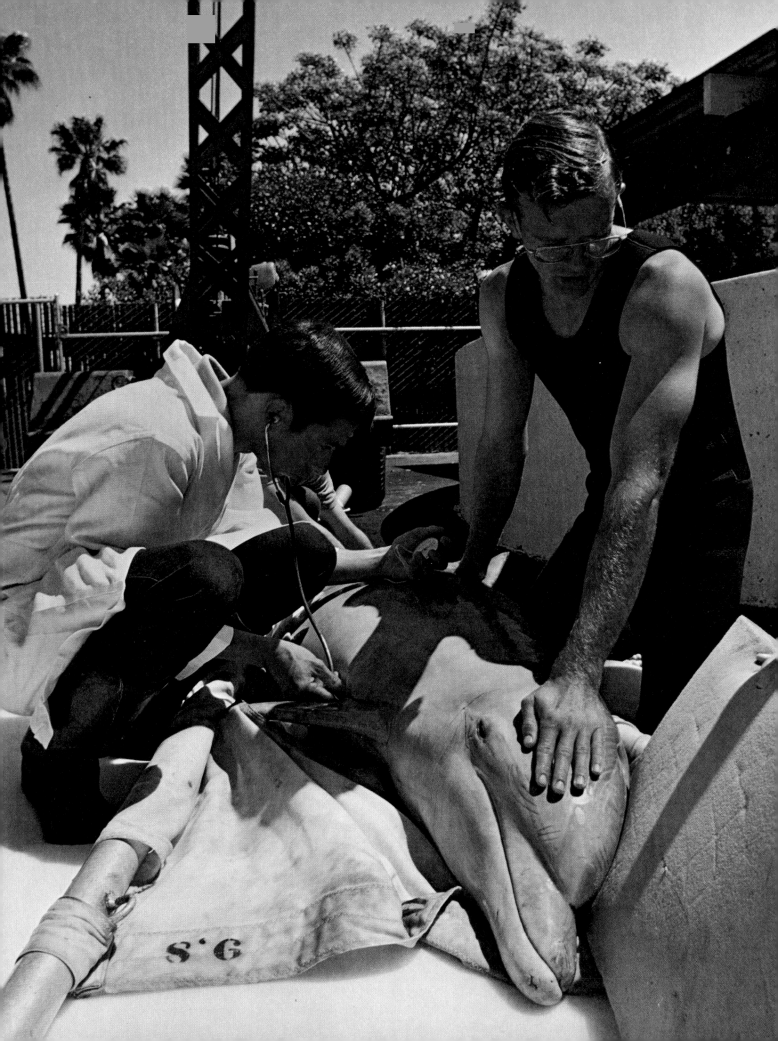

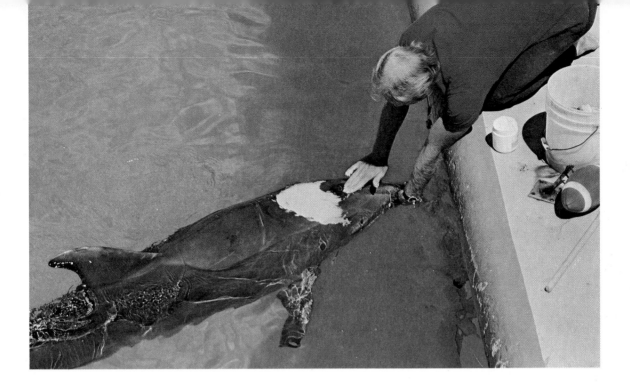

Dolphins get good care in oceanariums.
When a dolphin goes to a doctor, it rides in a big stretcher.
It can stay out of the water for a while if its skin is kept wet.
The doctor checks the dolphin and listens to its heart.
A cream keeps a dolphin's skin from getting sunburned or dry.
Every morning dolphins get vitamins that are hidden in their fish.
They go down in a big gulp. Most dolphins swallow fish whole.
They use their teeth only to catch fish—not to chew them.

Would you like to ride a dolphin?
Dolphins are fast, strong swimmers. They move their tails up and down to swim through the water.
A trainer balances on the backs of two speeding dolphins.
The girl zooms along as she holds onto a dolphin's fin.
Which ride do you think would be the most fun?

A trainer covers
Pebbles' eyes for a game.
He throws out rings
for her to find in the water.

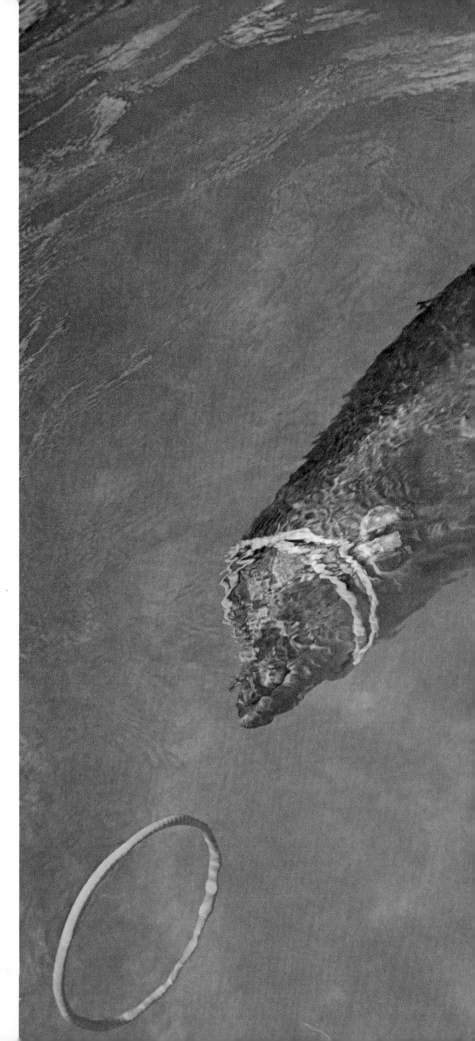

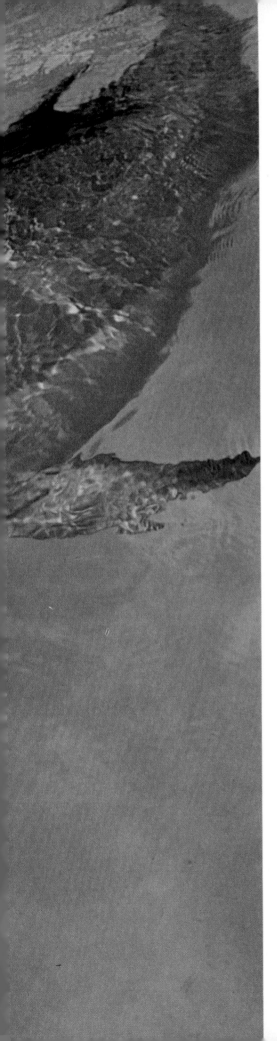

Pebbles cannot see.
How will she find the rings?
She will find them by making clicking sounds
as she swims through the water.
CLICK, CLICK, CLICK.
When the clicks hit a ring, the echoes
bounce back to her — *click, click, click.*
When Pebbles hears the echo-clicks,
she swims toward them and finds the ring.
Pebbles clicks some more. She quickly finds
the other rings and brings them to her trainer.
Dolphins use these clicks
to help find fish in the ocean.

Nellie carries a basketball in her flippers
and tail-walks from the end of the pool.
She brings the ball to her trainer.

Nellie is a star basketball player.
She puts her snout under the ball. WHOOSH!
The ball goes right into the basket.
Dolphins like to throw things.
They can pitch baseballs and toss footballs.
They will even throw things that they find
in the water, like feathers or fish.
If you play catch with a dolphin,
you might get a little wet. But it's fun!

Dolphins are great

jumpers—upside-down in a flip, through a ring, over a rope, or up for a fish.

Would you like to feed and pet a dolphin?
A dolphin's skin feels like a wet rubber ball.
Dolphins play a lot. One dolphin chases and splashes a sea gull.
Look at the faces of the dolphins in this book.
Their wide, curved mouths give them big smiles.
Dolphins usually act the way they look—playful and happy.

Happy birthday, Nellie!
Nellie celebrates her 23rd birthday
in the oceanarium
where she was born.

Apo rolls over
on her back
and waves goodbye
at the end of a show.

Published by The National Geographic Society
Robert E. Doyle, *President;* Melvin M. Payne, *Chairman of the Board;*
Gilbert M. Grosvenor, *Editor;* Melville Bell Grosvenor, *Editor-in-Chief*
Prepared by
The Special Publications Division
Robert L. Breeden, *Editor*
Donald J. Crump, *Associate Editor*
Philip B. Silcott, *Senior Editor*
Cynthia Russ Ramsay, *Managing Editor*
Elizabeth W. Fisher, *Research*
Wendy G. Rogers, *Communications Research Assistant*
Illustrations
David R. Bridge, *Picture Editor*
Josephine B. Bolt, *Art Director*
Cynthia Breeden, *Design Assistant*
Drayton Hawkins, *Design and Layout Assistant*
Production and Printing
Robert W. Messer, *Production Manager*
George V. White, *Assistant Production Manager*
Raja D. Murshed, June L. Graham, Christine A. Roberts, *Production Assistants*
John R. Metcalfe, *Engraving and Printing*
Jane H. Buxton, Stephanie S. Cooke, Mary C. Humphreys, Suzanne J. Jacobson,
Marilyn L. Wilbur, Linda M. Yee, *Staff Assistants*
Consultants
Dr. Kenneth S. Norris, University of California, Santa Cruz, *Scientific Consultant*
Dr. Glenn O. Blough, Peter L. Munroe, *Educational Consultants*
Edith K. Chasnov, *Reading Consultant*
The National Geographic Society thanks the staffs of the following oceanariums for their cooperation:
Marineland of Florida, St. Augustine, Florida; Marineland of the Pacific, Palos Verdes Peninsula,
California; Sea Life Park, Makapuu Point, Hawaii; Sea World, San Diego, California.
Illustrations Credits
All photographs by Lowell Georgia except: Lewis W. Walker (2-3); Linda M. Bridge,
National Geographic staff (12 top); Bill Huck, Marine Studios (24 bottom left).